YOUR KNOWLEDGE HAS VALUE

Vrushab Randive, Shubham Vernekar, Chandrasen Kumakar, Monika Shirbhate

3D Android Game Development with A.I

GRIN Publishing

Bibliographic information published by the German National Library:

The German National Library lists this publication in the National Bibliography;
detailed bibliographic data are available on the Internet at http://dnb.dnb.de .

Imprint:

Copyright © 2015 GRIN Verlag GmbH
Print and binding: Books on Demand GmbH, Norderstedt Germany
ISBN: 978-3-656-93199-7

GRIN - Your knowledge has value

Since its foundation in 1998, GRIN has specialized in publishing academic texts by students, college teachers and other academics as e-book and printed book. The website www.grin.com is an ideal platform for presenting term papers, final papers, scientific essays, dissertations and specialist books.

Visit us on the internet:

http://www.grin.com/

http://www.facebook.com/grincom

http://www.twitter.com/grin_com

3D ANDRIOD GAME DEVELOPMENT WITH A.I

Vrushab Randive Shubham Vernekar, Chandrasen Kumakar, Monika Shirbhate

Developer,Developer,Developer,Developer

Computer Department

G.H. RAISONI INSTITUTE OF ENGINEERING AND TECHNOLGY,PUNE,INDIA

Abstract — **this paper's study is the development of the mobile phone game based on Android OS. In this paper, we present the design and implementation of an Android game we will develop, called Sammy. In this game the player will select between available tiles to create a path for Sammy to reach to his home from school. Sammy is developed for mobile devices with the Android mobile operating system. The tool used for developing this game is Unity 3D game engine. The game will also have an A.I. player which the player can play against. Nowadays mobile gaming market is growing rapidly and is expected to be a $16 billion business by 2016. Almost all Android devices will be able to successfully run the game. We hope that sharing our experiences will assist others who wish to either use our mobile game or develop their own. Our research seeks to adding values and enjoyment to users of the Android mobile devices.   Key Words: Game Engines; Animation; Scripting; Android;**

I. Introduction

The game Sammy is developed for mobile devices with an Android operating system, which was designed as an operating system for mobile devices by Google and the Open Handset Alliance based on the Linux kernel. The game Sammy is a strategy game that lets player select and place a number of tiles to form a path from Sammy's school to his house. The game has two game modes (Predefined levels and VS. A.I.) And three levels of difficulty (easy, intermediate, and hard). Each tile will have its own unique specialties and the player has to strategize to find the best path for maximum score. Score will be awarded on the basis of time spent to complete the level, the number of tiles used and collecting stars. Each level will have 3 stars which will give bonus to the player.

Casual gamers tend to enjoy simple, yet dynamic games that are easy to understand, frequently reward the player, are short in duration (as opposed to games where

characters must be developed and nurtured), and have high re-playability by not becoming boring or repetitive. Our game achieves all these goals by adding new game play features and tiles as the level progresses.

1.1   Product Features

A high level list of the major features of our developed game is as follows.

- Two operational modes: single player and Vs. A.I.
- Three tiers of difficulty: easy, intermediate, and hard
- Invalid placements are not allowed.
- In-game rule-set, tutorial mode where the rules of the game are explained.
- Intuitive and linear interface.
- Smooth animation system.
- Bright, vibrant colors.

1.2   User Interface

Usability and portability are the most important quality attributes applicable to this research project. Since the game Sammy is targeted toward casual gamers, the interface and mechanics of game play are required to be simple and straight forward. Upon initial launch, the game enters *the* main screen, where the user can select one of the game modes (Single player and Vs. A.I.) or mess with the settings such as change volume or change difficulty. After game mode the system has enough information to initialize the game and allow game play to begin. Game play State is not a single state but an aggregation of several states like selection of tiles, placing of tiles, scoring. Upon completion of game play, the system transitions to the *End Game State*, where the user is notified of his success or failure. When the user does an invalid placement of tiles he will be notified of invalid movements, he will see a text message appear in a notification area after an invalid placement attempt.

1

II. Literature Survey

- Study of Unity 3D game engine for use of its physics and texture engines
- Use of MAYA and Adobe Photoshop for model and background design
- Nowadays many big companies have developed huge and interesting android games that have set the bar high
- In this independent game with our limited resources we will attempt to recreate the same spark as games developed by these big games.

III. Game engines

A game engine is a software framework designed for the creation and development of video games.

The core functionality typically provided by a game engine includes

1. Rendering engine ("renderer") for 2D or 3D graphics
2. Physics engine or collision detection
3. Animation
4. Scripting
5. A. I. and networking and much more

Fig 1. Logo of Frostbite Game Engine
[image courtesy/source:
http://wegotthiscovered.com/gaming/ea-bringing-frostbite-engine-mobile-platforms-skipping-wii/]

4.1. Unity - Game Engine

Unity is a game development ecosystem: a powerful rendering engine fully integrated with a complete set of intuitive tools and rapid workflows to create interactive 3D and 2D content.

Unity provides all the tools a game developer need to develop a 2D or 3D game on multiple platforms with minimum cost and time which makes it ideal for independent developers like us.

Fig 2. Logo of Unity Game Engine
[image courtesy/source:
http://imgkid.com/unity-3d-logo-png.shtml]

IV. Android Operating System

Android is a comprehensive operating environment that based on Linux® V2.6 kernel, it is also a layered system, the architecture of Android system is shown in the picture

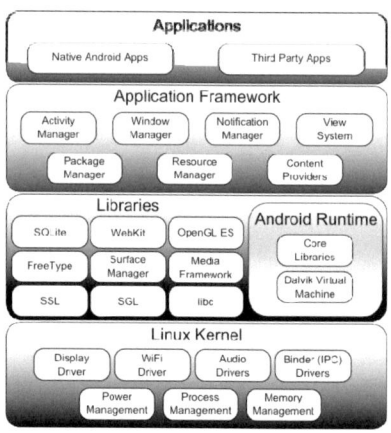

Fig 3. Architecture of Android
[image courtesy/source:
http://www.techotopia.com/index.php/An_Overview_of_th
e_Kindle_Fire_Android_Architecture]

Applications layer is the site of all Android applications including an email client, SMS program, maps, browser, contacts, and others. All applications are written using the Java programming language. Application framework layer defined the Android application framework. All Android applications are based on the application framework. The Android application framework including:

• A rich and extensible set of Views that can be used to build an application with beautiful user interface, including lists, grids, text boxes, buttons, and even an embeddable web browser.

• A set of Content Providers that enable applications to access data from other applications (such as Contacts), or to share their own data.

• A Resource Manager that provides access to non-code resources such as localized strings, graphics, and layout files.

• A Notification Manager that enables all applications to display custom alerts in the status bar.

• An Activity Manager that manages the lifecycle of applications and provides a common navigation back stack.

Libraries layer includes a set of C/C++ libraries used by various components of the Android system and provides support to the application framework. [2]

V. Algorithms

These are the algorithms used in our project for the two game modes and also the behavior of A.I.

6.1. Algorithm

1. The game will start with a GUI allowing player to
    1. Compete against A.I. opponent
    2. Try to beat predefined levels and set high scores
    3. Mess with game setting such as sound on or off
2. When a new game is started the game will generate a level which will be a n*m size board (where n = no of rows and m = no of columns) made of square tiles.
3. Each of these levels will have a predefined starting point tile and an ending point tile
4. Each level will also have 3 stars on tiles which when obtained will give special points
5. The player will be given a set of tiles to choose from and objective of the player is to take the object from the starting point to the finish point in least time and most score
6. Each tile will have special properties and it's the players task to choose the best combination of these tiles to get the most score
7. After player has decided the path the game will show the simulation of the object going from the start point to the end
8. At the end of level player will be shown various statistics about his/her performance.
9. The player will be advanced to next level and a new level will be generated

6.2. Algorithm: Predefined Levels

Here each level will have a starting tile and a finish tile.

1. Each level will also feature some predefined tiles that must be used by the player and 3 stars which will grant bonus score.
2. The objective of the player is to take the object from start tile to end tile and try to make the highest score
3. The player will be allowed to choose from a set of tiles to form a path to take the object from start to finish
4. Once all tiles are selected the object will be released from start tile and pass through the various tiles
5. Each tile will have its own effect on the path of the object
6. If the player manages to take the object to a tile with a star then bonus score will be added
7. If the object reaches the finish tile then the level is completed and the score is given according to the time taken and the number of tiles used

8. Each tile will have a unique score to it
9. Once the level is completed the next level will be loaded
10. Some levels will also have additional objectives like
    1. Speed traps
    2. Time limits
    3. Limited tiles etc.

6.3. Algorithm: Versus A.I.

Here each level will have a starting tile and a finish tile

1. Each level will also feature some predefined tiles that must be used by the player and 3 stars which will grant bonus score
2. The objective of the player is to take the object from start tile to end tile and try to the beat the score of made by the game A.I.
3. The player will be allowed to choose from a set of tiles to form a path to take the object from start to finish
4. Once all tiles are selected the game will choose their own tiles with the A.I algorithm and show them to the player
5. After seeing the A.I. arrangement the player will be allowed to alter any one of its tiles
6. Once the player is ready both the object will be released from start tile and pass through the various tiles
7. Each tile will have its own effect on the path of the object
8. The two objects will not collide with each other
9. If the player manages to take the object to a tile with a star then bonus score will be added but the star will only be awarded to the object that first reaches the star
10. If both objects reach the star at same time then both will get bonus score
11. If the object reaches the finish tile then the match is completed and the score is given according to the time taken and the number of tiles used
12. Each tile will have a unique score to it
13. The score of A.I and Player is compared and the winner will be declared as the one with the most score

3

14. Some levels will also have other criteria for comparison like
    1. Speed traps at certain tiles
    2. Time Taken to finish
    3. Slowest to finish wins etc.

6.4. Algorithm: A.I. Algorithm

1. Start
2. For each type of tile make relations to all the other tiles and store a compatibility score for each relation
3. All tiles will also have an initiating score which is how suitable the tile is to start the game
4. All tiles will also have special physics constraints that will reduce misplacement of compatible tiles
5. Using the initiating score the first tile will be laid among the available tiles.
6. After the first tile is laid, compatibility scores will be used to find the most suitable three tiles for the next step
7. A random tile among these three tiles will be selected
8. After all tiles are selected the game will perform a virtual run
9. If the virtual run is unsuccessful then go to step 5
10. If the virtual run is successful then show the tile arrangement to the player and game will run on these tiles to set score to beat for the player

VI. Mathematical Model

7.1. Problem Definition

Let 'G' be the Game System that

$G = \{R, C, A, S, AI, B, Sp, Pr,T, Sc, IP\}$

R- Rendering engine $\qquad R = \{R_1, R_2, R_3,...Rn\}$

C- Collision engine $\qquad R = \{C_1, C_2, C_3,...Cn\}$

A- Animation $\qquad A = \{A_1, A_2, A_3,...An\}$

Engine may vary according to the unity S/W

S- Scripting $\{S_1, S_2, S_n\}$

Also specify the language used

CF Core functionality $= \{R, C, A, S, AI\}$

AI – Artificial Intelligence

D- Display along with GUI

Tile generator $\{t_1, t_2, ... t_n\}$

L- Levels $\{L_1, L_2, L_3, ... L_n\}$

B- Board of size $\{n*m\}$

Speed- $Sp = \{Sp_1, Sp_2,... Sp_n\}$ depends on tiles

P- Period/ time of the Game i.e. Length of the level

T- No. of tiles $\{t_1, t_2,... t_n \}$

Pr - Parameters

It includes

Difficulty

Length

Obstacles

type

$Pr = \{D, L, O, T\}$

D- $\{D_1, D_2,...D_n\}$ Level of difficulties

L- $\{L_1, L_2,... L_n\}$ Length of the level of tile

O- $\{O_1, O_2,... O_n\}$ Obstacles in a tile

Type = T- $\{T_1, T_2,... T_n\}$

Sc – Scores

Sc- $\{Sc_1, Sc_2,...Sc_n\}$

e.g. 3 star bonus

IP- Input -> touch

i.e. movement of touch

Left, Right, Up, Down, Teleport, Bomb, Ice, Lava

7.2. Generalized Domain

It is a part of Reinforcement learning

On every time step the agent/ user must select an action in discrete 3D action space.

e.g.: dim 1 $\{-1, 0, 1\}$

Used for left or right movement

dim 2 $\{0, 1\}$

Jump/ Not jump

dim3 $\{0, 1\}$

Walking/ Running

4

This 3D action space can be considered as action space of distinct actions.

User receives state information from tiles as a 21 x 16 array of tiles shows a state space corresponding to the view of game.

Tile: Tells info about object. Can travel through tile, if it can walk on top of the tile, etc.

Action value function Q -> rewards

7.3. Markov decision processes (MDPs)

Defines 4 tuples

MDP = {S, A, T, R}

S -> State

A -> Action

T -> Transition function : Game engine will take care of its working

R-> Rewards: Game engine will handle its working

State:

User/ agent precieves the current state

SES (possible with noise)

Levels are episodic-

i.e. agent dies/ completes a level so it includes agent actions it may or reset to level that is next

Action: A

Action available to the agent/ user

T: Transition function

$T: S \times A \to S$

i/p = takes S & A as i/p & returns the state of the environment after action is performed

Goal of agent=Maximize its reward/ scores. Scores are represented using

Scalar values defined for reward function. $R = S \to R$

T & S are controlled by game engine

7.4. User learning

Actions to take in state the policy.

$\Pi: S \to A$

Π: Modified by learner over time to improve performance defined as expected total reward/ score

$Q: S \times A \to R$ (Π learning using temporal difference method). Optimal action from any state by executing the action with highest action value function.

As the state grows it can be stored in Table format of Q and Π. But it is impossible to store them in the table form is the state space is continuous using State variable

$$S = \{x1, x2,...xn\}$$

sSo this issue is resolved using tile coding, AI, discretization

7.5. Morphism

In game "G" there are many objects interacting with each other through functions. Here we make use of Petri net.

Petri net is a 3-tuple (B,E,F)

Where,

B= non-null set of conditions

E= set of events

F C= (B*E) U(E*B) is the causal dependency relation that satisfy the restrictions

{b E B | e F b} are non-null for all events e E E.

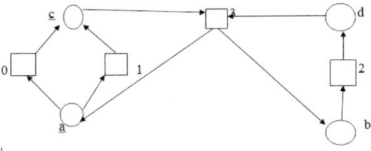

Fig 4. Flow relations:

Definition:

Let N1= (B1, E1, F1, M1) be the nets for i= 0, 1

Defines a morphism of nets for N0 to N1 to be a pair of relations (η, β) with $\eta <= E0 \times E1$, a partial function and $B <= B0 \times B1$ such that:

1) N1=βN1 and γ

2) If b0βb1 then η ('bo x 'b1) is a total function 'bo $\longrightarrow$ b 1

3) If e0 η ex then ('ex *ey) is a total function ei->e0

And η (b0' xb1') is a total function b0' $\longrightarrow$ b1'

If further η is total we say the morphism (η,β) is synchronous. When η and β are total functions we say the morphism (η,β) is a folding. When η and β are the inclusion relations η:E0<=E1 and β:B0 C=B1 we says N0 is a subnet of N1.

Subnet provide the simplest examples of morphism on nets. They have a simple characterization and arise naturally by restricting a net to a subset of events.

Proposition:

Let N0=(B0, E0,F0,M0) and N1=(B1,E1,F1,M1) be nets. Then N0 is a subnet of N1if B0C= B1, E0 C= E1, M0 = M1 and

Proposition:

Let N=(B,E,F,M) be a net. Let E' C= E. Define the restriction of N to E', written N|E', to be (B, E', F',M) where F'=F ((B x E') U (E' x B)).

The restriction N|E' is a subnet of N.

7.6. Activities

Activity A1: Start game

First, the player will select between predefined levels or versus A.I mode

Activity A2: Assembly of engine with core functionality

Assembly of tiles according to levels

Activity A3: Agent vs. AI

Player will now play against AI

Activity A4: Validation of levels

All the tiles will be organized properly and game is set to start

Activity A5: Score calculation

Scores will be calculated

Activity A6: Highest scores

Managing high scores of user

VII. Conclusion

Android as a full, open and free mobile device platform, with its powerful function and good user experience rapidly developed into the most popular mobile operating system. Here we give an introduction of Android and developing games for android.
Today developing android apps and publishing them has been easier than ever. There are millions of android devices in the market and are increasing by the day
MORE DEVICES = MORE DEMAND FOR APPS
Android games are today an important part of most peoples leisure lives and increasingly an important part of our culture as a whole.

VIII. References

[1] Sergey Karakovskiy and Julian Togelius, *"The Mario AI Benchmark and Competitions"* member, ieee, ieee transactions on computational intelligence and ai in games, vol. 4, no. 1, march 2012

[2] Justin R. Martinez, 1 Wenbin *"The Design and Implementation of an Android Game: Foxes and Chicken"* Luo2 Vol.3, Issue.2, March-April. 2013 pp-1129-1134

[3] Philipp Svoboda, Wolfgang Karner, Markus Rupp *"Traffic Analysis and Modeling for World of Warcraft"* reviewed at the direction of IEEE Communications Society subject matter experts for publication in the ICC 2007

[4] Jianye Liu Jiankun Yu *"Research on Development of Android Applications"* 2011 Fourth International Conference on Intelligent Networks and Intelligent Systems